LIT ANGELS

Margaret Saine

Moonrise Press

LIT ANGELS

Margaret Saine

Moonrise Press

This book is published by Moonrise Press
P.O. Box 4288, Los Angeles – Sunland
CA 91041-4288, www.moonrisepress.com
info@moonrisepress.com

© Copyright 2017 by Margaret Saine and Moonrise Press.

© Cover art by Maja Trochimczyk, based on a photograph by Margaret Saine. Used by Permission.

Illustrated with ten photographs by Margaret Saine. Used by Permission.

All Rights Reserved 2017 by Moonrise Press

No part of this book may be reproduced or utilized in any form or by any means, electronic or mechanical, including photocopying and recording, or by any information storage and retrieval system, without permission in writing from the publisher.

Manufactured in the United States of America

The Library of Congress Publication Data:

Saine, Margaret
[Poems. English, with translations into German, French, Arabic and Italian]
Lit Angels / Margaret Saine, author
96 pages (xiv pp. + 82 pp.) 15.2 cm x 22.9 cm. Written in English.
    Includes original poems, with some German, French, Arabic, and Italian translations, as well as 14 photos by the author, and her portrait.
    ISBN 978-1-945938-02-3 (paperback)
    ISBN 978-1-945938-04-7 (color paperback)
    ISBN 978-1-945938-05-4 (ebook in ePub format)
    I. Saine, Margaret – Poetry. II. Title.

10 9 8 7 6 5 4 3 2 1

*lit
angels
or lit angles
corners literal
with an easychair
light
and
a book
literature angles
or angels
engines
[all in a whisper]
when we can see life
brightly lit
life's spirit
in the bluest part
of our mind
in liquid
light*

*For D. H., a friend in need,
and when it all became words, a friend indeed*

Are angels there?
   ~ Edward Young

Poetry is language at its most distilled and most powerful.
~ Rita Dove

A poem is a flame,
ranging all the way
from straw fire
to conflagration.
~ Berta Nimetz

Poetry: the best words in the best order.
~ Samuel Taylor Coleridge

If I read a book and it makes my whole body
so cold no fire can ever warm me,
I know that is poetry.
~ Emily Dickinson

Everything one invents is true,
you may be perfectly sure of that.
Poetry is as precise as geometry.
~ Gustave Flaubert

Breathe in experience, breathe out poetry.
~ Muriel Rukeyser

> Poetry is the mother-tongue of the human race.
> ~ *Johann Georg Hamann*

...and the will becomes again
a garden. The poem
is complex
and the place made
in our lives
for the poem.
~ *William Carlos Williams*

> Poetry is thoughts that breathe, and words that burn.
> ~ Thomas Gray

And I wonder about
this lifetime with myself,
this dream I'm living.
~ *Anne Sexton*

> *Je suis à qui m'a compris.~*
> *I belong to whoever understands me.*
> ~ *Jules Michelet*

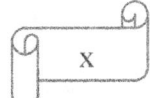

Contents

Words ~ 1
    Inside ~ 2
    Made Without Hands ~ 3
    Words in the Night ~ 5
    Bridges ~ 6
    My Rainbow ~ 7
    Your Name Here ~ 8
    From Darkness to Lightning ~ 9
    It Takes Nine Days—Nine 140-Keystroke Poems ~ 10
    Names ~ 13

Life ~ 15
    Corporal ~ 16
    Crows ~ 18
    Threads ~ 19
    Face ~ 21
    Alive — Lebendig ~ 22
    Balm and Candle ~ 23
    A Greek Orthodox Angel ~ 24
    Consenting ~ 25
    Fire ~ 26
    Anatomy — A Pantoum ~ 27
    Angels and Angles ~ 28
    Yours Concupiscently ~ 29
    Body Memory ~ 30
    Twenty-Four Hours ~ 31
    Wondering ~ 32
    Long Walk ~ 34
    A Voice ~ 35
    The Tree Outside ~ 36

Pain ~ 37
    Agamemnon ~ 38
    Ivan the Terrible ~ 40

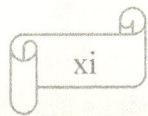

The Charleston Massacre ~ 41
Exile Everywhere Exile ~ 42
Impermanence — Impermanenza ~ 43
Night and Light ~ 44

Water ~ 45

Biomes ~ 46
By Wave Express ~ 47
Travel Brochure ~ 49
Even in the Rain ~ 51
As I Look Back ~ 52
Aunt ~ 53
Unraveled—Sfilacciata ~ 54
Travel Envy ~ 56
Like A Reed ~ 57
Writing On Water ~ 58
Music of Reflected Light ~ 60

Paintings ~ 61

Transplant ~ 62
Joaquin Sorolla ~ 63
Titian-Titans at Work ~ 64
Giorgio Morandi ~ 65
Munch's New Snow ~ 66
Munch's Winter ~ 67
Klee's Moonlight ~ 68
Brancusi's Sleeping Muse ~ 69
Diebenkorn's Tomatoes ~ 70
Constable Says ~ 74

Last Songs ~ 73

The Quasida of Creations ~ 74
Curtain Call ~ 75
Ulalume Gonzalez De Leon ~ 76
Horizons ~ 77
Breadcrumbs ~ 78
Early Spring ~ 79

Preface

Literature Angels ~ Angels of Light

Poems of 2014 and 2015

Lit, past participle of 'to light', and Lit, abbreviation for literature? Lit used by people who love it so much they breathlessly shorten it to one syllable? Light and Literature, the mainstays of human lives, wherever we are, whenever we are so privileged. Literature and Light are best friends. But especially here, in the City of Angels, my chosen home [German 'Wahlheimat'], Light and Literature, where people of vastly different origins, cultures, and religions try to get along. I'm part of this world, and I want to be. World Peace for Dummies? Maybe such a book should be written. And I am working on it. In the meantime, poetry can only describe the margins of sadness and joy, where essays cannot reach.

~ *Margaret Saine*

WORDS

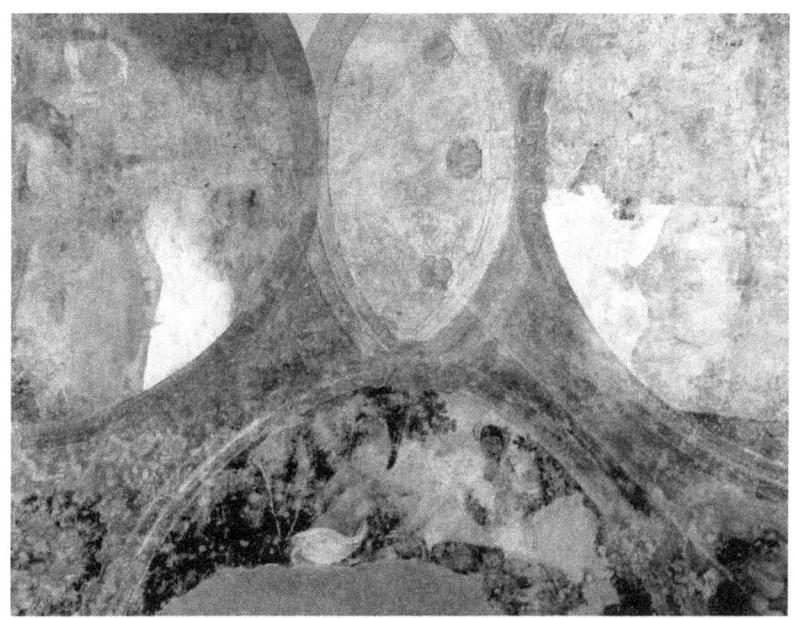

Inside

A line will take us hours maybe
~ William Butler Yeats

I have a poem stuck
inside this computer
it rests and sleeps
in a cluster of words
a skein of memories
its second nature coagulating
like grains of sand slowly
but surely becoming a pearl

Its first nature — words
pieces of migrant beauty
in a life of theirs won
by their own becoming
honed to a purpose
polished until the poem
says to me in its own mirror
what it says: a moment or thought
wrapped in a word

I call to the poem in her cradle
I wake 'to whom it may concern'
from her sleep to read me
I open windows
to call on her words to breathe
so we may resume what concerns us
the day's work and the field work
the light and dark shifting
at the window where they turn
into words: poems in action

Perhaps a book? Walking into an angel
perhaps, and exiting?
Exciting yes, exiting never

Made Without Hands

~ to my friend, the Italian poet Rita Stanzione

Your poem
— is it or isn't it —
made without hands?

So it is not
an a-cheiro-poieton
you say?

Words that weren't there before
as you were not there
- as I wasn't here -
just a moment ago

All of a sudden there it came
there they were
words in the air
did they fly google-carried
in through the window?

And then you had it in your hands
your hands at a world
of words within reach
at the touch of your hands

The truth is
it fell into your hands
and you received the poem
gently as a newborn

And yes it is
down-to-earth
it's a hand-made
hands-on inspiration

It's your poem
lips moving
and it has won
its own being

P.S. *Acheiropoieton [αχειροπόιετον]* something not made by human hands, but by inspiration, such as a poem, whereas contradictorily the Greek word *"poiema"* means *"what has been made"*, but does not specify how.

Words in the Night

In the night
the words
the touches and the smiles
are still inside

Words I'm prepared
to remember
to ruminate even
until they convince

Night brings us
our own ghosts

In the night
words are swimming
upstream in dreams
dripping drops of light

And the stars in my eyes
dark seas inside us
shine for you deep

This love still inside
cannot hide
Not even
inside the night

Come morning
it steps outside
and bursts out of its seams
windows open wide
it stumbles out into the sun
and like her it beams

Bridges

The bent backrest of a chair
a bridge
the dry arched leaf scraping on the ground
a bridge
an arch of masonry
bridge
a runway curve
is a bridge
a Romanesque vault
see the bridge up there
a balustrade with statues
the bow of a mountain range

Your words and mine
best bridge there is

My Rainbow

I hide out
in the green forest
of your words
in the shade of shadows

to find you
I find my purple self
perhaps a dream

I remain speechless
our multicolored hands touch
lonely and alive
we change our colors to orange
in the embracing breeze

as we follow
a fog of veiled yellows
of floating whys
lepidopteral maybes
ever changing hues

colorful words darting out
buzzing butterflies
chameleon tongues
embrace as we embrace
in the gentle breeze
of the sunset

Your Name Here

When hunted
lizards drop their tails
when you believed yourself hunted
you numbly or nimbly
dropped your name in your wake

It's not made of china
it will not break
so cut it to keep it
from sticking

Someone may want it
loose and lost by the wayside
a tarnished piece of skin
detached from the golden goose

You dropped your name
you left behind a ghost
unwittingly outwitted it
and ran for your life
which no one wanted to take

But now you got away with another
without any murder, see?
Now you can afford to drop in
on other names unrecognized
and wait for the coming breakup
of others when you might want to
escape again from your name

From Darkness to Lightning

> *For poetry makes nothing happen: it survives*
> *In the valley of its saying.* ~ *W. H. Auden*

I wish to respect
the darkness that's inside you

The inner core of your shade
your own dark continent

The geology of your body and heart
the hidden strata of your earth

Where all your growing takes place
the depth of your caves

The rumors and the silences
the bottom of your seas

The inside of your clouds
the twirling winds

Your inner electric storms
appearing as lightning

When You Enlightened
becomes Enlightened Me

It Takes Nine Days to Fall
From Heaven to Earth

These poems were smuggled out of a regime where all poems, including love poems, must have 140 or fewer keystrokes. But mostly they have not fewer, they have exactly 140: people will squeeze their emotions in all the way to the last letter.

    Trees start the wind
    a tussle of warm and cold
    in foliage of light and shadow
    interwoven bodies
    sighing and softly groaning
    trees start the music
    140

    A relation is not
    written in chalk
    nor with a ballpoint
    or a blue fountain pen
    A relation is
    a declaration of faith
    oftentimes torpedoed
    by chance
    140

    Where are we
    when we are here?
    Both here, we think?
    Or are we not?
    Then where are we?
    And then suddenly

the picture goes blank
the room is empty
140

Someone's not here
someone is always leaving
then someone's coming back
that's another story
maybe a changed person
stuck with
the nonce word life
140

What's mountain in you
and valley in me
may turn round
in earth-shaking embrace
to valley of you
a mountain of me
wheeling bodies
open to the sky
140

It's so easy
to deify the moment
and also deify chance
those are the dice
that fortune has thrown us
and in those rare moments
we are truly happy
140

I would have enjoyed life
as a book end
except books don't end
unless you'd run out of shelf
space in the depths of the
continental shelf inside
140

The language of birds
a speaking in tongues
to clouds and the sky
of which we share
a fraction—
the whisper of a sound
an inkling of mere music
140

We happily found
as a word to be treasured
picked up and
pressed to the heart
read silent and loudly:
happiness of the world
encapsulated in a word
140

According to a Greek myth, it takes nine days to fall from heaven to earth.

Names

Ratisbona
Strasburgo
Augusta
Stoccarda
Basilea

Amberes
Aquisgrán
Burdeos
Tolosa

Eu-ropa
is a good one
Names like caresses
first heard by
Renaissance diplomats
and merchants
pouring South
across the Aps
and the Pyrenees
a Southern sound
more florid
than the original

To remind us of
our Europeanness
And we love back
what's south of the Alps
and the Pyrenees
but their names
are already perfect

What's in a name
asks Juliet
names are caresses
like pinning a rose
and a violet
on your lapel, Juliet

Just think about it
that's also Europe
our Europe
Be happy, my good Eu-ropa!

LIFE

Corporal

The bruises that the stick
wrote on my child's hand
the brutality of fact
red streaks surrounded
by black and blue skin
made me wonder
what I had done

They stuck to me
as ghosts
images and cognates
of myself
as if they were some ink
the black and the blue
that my body, a reverse squid
slowly devoured and excised
from my life
regurgitating into making them
sight unseen

Or thinking later
if I might use this ink
to write my life
within the limits
of my knowledge
feeling the pain
I never failed to feel
but now doing the obverse
eating cuttlefish ink
risotto di nero di seppia

in Rome
merluza en tinta de sepia
in Bilbao
encre de poulpe or seiche
whenever it was offered

To tell the world
to reinforce the real story
to let the stick stick
that I could only understand
as cruel and unusual punishment
brutality of fact

Crows

I
Sightings
Life and love
in a sunny triumph
of delicious indulgence
lived or imagined

II
She will smile
like flashes of light
flitting through leaves
light and dark
with the wind

III
And yet she wants
to take exception to
the caw caw of the crows
flying overhead

IV
And then again their speech
reminds her of wisdom
varieties of abandon
and memories
anticipating winter days
of deep thoughts ahead

V
She will be queen
who sees the most birds.
      — *Italian proverb*

Threads

She holds in her fingers
a thread and wraps it
around her index
unwraps it into an untidy skein
a warp to rewrap it again

Her right fingers stroke
the fingers of her left hand
a wind ruffling the fronds of palms
playfully subsiding
and starting up again
when warm and cold air clash
to play their life game as wind

Women having to do with threads
Ariadne Penelope and many others
and *we* today
Sappho Cassandra and Pythia
hold their word threads
in the foretold sequence: the burden of words
in a necklace of beads
a rosary none other
of pain and sorrow
told to male poets

Plump vowels dissected
by sputtering consonants
speech bubbles erupting like pearls
emerge from a deep-conch sea
crunched to expel them

To make us gasp
and grasp the meaning
stories as spacers
pacemakers of life
—read peacemakers—
there for us to accept with a smile
the stoking of warming fires but contained

And in the news today
'Unidentified amnesiac woman
found today in California'

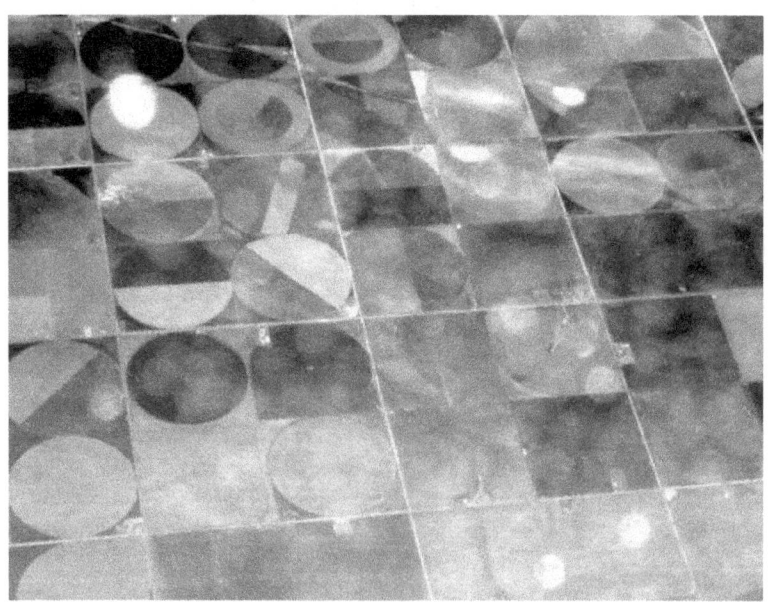

Face

I search for a face
where there is none
there never has been
unless I've
perhaps imagined

Eyes closed in reverie
lashes as if pages in a book
the smooth cheekbones
a smoky furrowed brow
rebellious grey curls
bare ecstatic eye sockets
a nonchalant cigarette
dangling from the
left corner of the mouth
[what is it
I thought you don't smoke?]

Museum or photo
or Internet
I want to find your face
to see myself
again and again
in your eyes
smoke or no smoke

Alive—Lebendig

Receive the pearl from the treadmill
~ Jane North

Morning alive—
no doubt—
        which tolerates
no comparative
    [aliver? alivest?]

To me
    you are alive
        as the sans serif
staccato bird call
    of the morning

Maybe it's only
    in the words
        we share

The sparks of life
    the specks of light
        this instant
that fly back and forth
    between us

Remember
    anything that's blue on top
        can be sky
            or heaven

Lebendig

Lebendiger Morgen—
        kein Zweifel—
              [er duldet
keinen Komparativ?]

Für mich
        bist du lebendig
              wie die Groteskschrift
Sans Serif
        der staccato Vogelsang
              am Morgen

Vielleicht ist es nur
        in den Worten
               die wir teilen

Die Lebensfunken
        Lichtflecken
              im Augenblick
die zwischen uns
        hin und her fliegen

Verrgiss nicht
        Alles was oben blau ist
              kann Himmel sein

Translated by Margaret Saine

Balm and Candle

Tout notre langage est composé de petits songes brefs.
All our language consists of small, short dreams.
~ Paul Valéry

I'm much too old
    to bother with beauty

And virtue names
    the all but incomprehensible

Only a dark forest
    will do for my longings

Only a language exposed
    and shining like teeth

When the banal finally
    starts teeming with curiosity

And your mental presence
    provides the healing touch

Amid tree crowns
    of balm and candle

The wakeful waves
    of wisely moving snakes

Where you will find at length
    this body of mine
        undulating with desire

Think of me as paper
    thin white and trembling

I want to be your poem
    Come and write me

Consenting

Cold air on my cheek
from the lowest setting of the fan
now almost as cool
as night air unventilated
which blows from the side
like a caress to make me smile

Growling airliner at a distance
flying over the lights of Orange County
along the wavy shoreline
of the Pacific, for sure a
night flight to Mexico City
the sinking rumbling sound
digging deeper and deeper
into the night until
sound and plane fall
below the horizon

Illegible stars
like weeds in the sky
if I don't learn them
and I musing about how much
or how little I want
— I still want it and when I want it —
to share with another person
wie die Katze um den heißen Brei
like the cat around the hot porridge

We are a natural ballet of two
a ball-and-chain linking and likeness
adults almost consenting
like a painting by Valentin
like Beatrice and Benedick
mutual desire intently watched
by each other's wry smile
and the guffaws of the rest
of the guys at the bar

Fire

You are a fire
to come at me
from the transparent distance
having traversed large
fireless provinces

Now the corrugated air
surrounds you in wobbly waves
and we play at combustion
whipped up by your winds
of a serious fury

I do not invoke
this fire in vain
You may not know
how you burn and sear
randomly all year around

You may need a plan
a goal
a furnace
a focus [meaning: little fire]

And matter to burn
char once and for all:
Here, take it,
it's my heart
I want to be part of
your dreaming fire

Anatomy — A Pantoum

I want you inside me
I want your musical unrest
But not just in my head
Not just stirring the heart
Until we lose hearing and sight

I want your musical unrest
I want you deep down there
I want to hold you there
I want to move the colors inside us

But not just in my head
To move us, you and me
Thrust us deep down
Where the sparks fly

Not just stirring the heart
But where a fire song is born
The ancient singsong psalm
From a blind spot of hearsay

Until we lose hearing and sight
Word for word and body for body
Until we rest our breaths
Holding them in a long fermata

Angels and Angles — A Dialog

— when we make love
we become angels

— yes, angels would be us
if they made love

— angels though sometimes
there are no angels
just angles

— let's reconsider
there are angles and curves
we are curves, mostly?

— I know I'm a curve
that wants to be fluid
enveloping you like water

— and I am a tangent
that wants to kiss you

— then let's be tangled tangents
leaving the hard sciences
to float among the clouds

— *Amico caro,*
is there a way to translate us
into the present tense?

Yours Concupiscently

~ to answer John Donne

Thou denie'st me nothing and so
on four urgent concupiscent lips
we dismiss the flea ambassador
for shame and we shamelessly kiss

Commingled our liquids be
so that our saps delighted flow
away to shores of lost virginity
with sandy waves beguilingly

Embracing us long ardent last
to kindle urgent feelings lost
Yet we in glorious havoc suck

In lively greed licentious nectar
from eager pores gasping for more
and ever more of our lucid lust

P. S. A bit of a contradiction, here's a sonnet about Donne, not in the British, but in the Petrarchan vein I am used to.

Body Memory

The body doesn't forget.
Not the touching.
Not the lying together
The moving as one
Cushions and pillows
as cloudy perspectives
The body doesn't forget
embraces like heaven
burning like
the fires of hell

Twenty-Four Hours

Twenty-four hours
of feeling beautiful
of never doubting myself

The cult you render
transports me to shores
of a placid ego
I've rarely glimpsed

In the shuffle of the years
I had gotten used to
the scars of living

To love or be loved
which is better? Both
at the same time

And I have only
you to thank
in the morning

Wondering

Our dreams float uncertain
up there in the clouds where
we can't see them
and still we dream on and on
and we wonder
do they size each other up
our dreams?
Might they commingle?
Might they talk to each other
and touch and speak and kiss?
Maybe...

We down here
we don't know
down here
we can't see
and we wonder and wait
and wait and wonder

Dreams please
make up your minds!
And be sure
to let us know!

Long Walk

I promenade
the thought of you
in my head
all over the continent
to riverbeds and seashores
piazzas and forests
churches and railroad stations

Thought that accompanies me
wherever I go
as eyes do eye charts
mustard does vinaigrette
and together we take
long excursions

Time is unlimited
but seems to endure
for now until the day
before we know it

But for now
I have the whole desert to cross
thinking thoughts about you

A Voice

How can you fall in love with a bird
maybe as the voice of someone
you hold dear in your heart but distant.
You long to get your hands

on her, your ears on her hazy voice.
Then in your other dealings
you forget the darling sounds
that promise to wound and heal

so that your daily life becomes
an unctuous and tortuous battle.
Until one day in the plaza

you hear that pristine voice again
from the bird cages of your search
which was a search for the right one.

The Tree Outside

Above the window sill
the minuscule stippled leaves
dance in the breeze

Mulberry trunk
cut by the window sill
as if as if—

By inner eye we know
the tree to be intact

Trunk reaches down to roots
where the atoms come from
roots and trunk
spread into sky
rhizomes breathing
the vital breath
that sustains us

PAIN

Agamemnon

I

A man slaying a female
in order to become victorious
what a thing
He chose his own daughter
Iphigenia stands at the altar
before men armed for slaughter
though the wind came up
on its own
to drown out her lament

II

Killing Iphigenia
with his own hands
drops of blood
sprinkling his clothes
puddling down
the steps of the temple
snaking into a deep pit
to be embraced
and redeemed by the earth

III

Only one death
and only a woman
but a heavy stain
on time and space

a blemish on memory
Agamemnon destined
for more killing
myriad bloodshed
of remote peoples

IV

And destined to be killed
Victorious returning from Troy
he falls slaughtered
by his own wife Electra

Ivan the Terrible

After Ivan the Terrible
killed his son
and killed thousands more
or had thousands killed
to unify Russia

Despite the cruelty
he had a Memorial Book
of his victims prepared
so that people would be able
to pray for the souls by name

His son's name
Ivan Ivanovich
was writ large
in this book of conscience

We do not know
if the Czar prayed for him
or had someone pray
we do not know
who prayed for the Czar
in the end

The Charleston Massacre

White people are trapped in a history they don't understand.
~ James Baldwin

To sneak into a church
and be embraced,
was it not enough?
To sing those hymns,
as if Moses had just
come down the mountain?
No, for you it was not enough:
you came with a gun.
Did no one teach you
the bloody cruelty
of suffering slaves?
The field slave
and the house slave
forever divided?
Teach of children sired
by the white man
on the black woman and
taken to slave market,
his chattel to sell?
Teach you who were the ones
who got rich, and by God,
it wasn't ever your white trash ancestors,
nor was it you. But why do you still
have to hate them so?
What have they done to you
except embrace you
and share their songs?
What have they done to you
that you haven't done worse to them?

Exile Everywhere Exile

What happens when people
mix and travel
when you go to a place
you very much admire
and meet someone from there
who tells you [a long story]
how he hates his homeland?
How could your dreams and desires
deflect his convictions
based on the real? They cannot.
Where do you both end up going
when he insists he does not want to stay
after he has destroyed
your hopes and aspirations of staying?
You cannot take his place
nor assume his fate but
meanwhile you have fallen in love
with him, making you a stranger,
an ever more landless, more impossible
unhappy dweller on this earth.
And a woman to boot.
What happens when two religions
share one holy place and each
—heedless of the other
except determined to slay—decides to fight for sole possession?
History is no help, nor is realpolitik,
two schemes from the netherworld.
By this time the argument
has absconded into the fanatic
no longer susceptible to persuasion.
And people of good will
are called to suffer again and again,
until they put an end to it
[if they can]

Impermanence—Impermanenza

Impermanence of the crystal
impermanence of cold
and of heat
Impermanence all the way
inside the rock
Impermanence from
any movement that
as a wind
of floating air
transports us elsewhere
where we are and become again
impermanence

Impermanenza del cristallo
impermanenza del freddo
e del calore
Impermanenza fino a
dentro la pietra
Impermanenza di ogni
movimento che
come un vento
d'aria fluttuante
ci transporta altrove
dove siamo e diventiamo di nuovo
impermanenza

Translated by Margaret Saine

Night— and Light?

> *Vivir quiero conmigo*
> *I want to live with myself*
> Fray Luis de León

Night is coming and so
the light vanishes but
many lights are born
into the dusk
into the dark
Night is the backdrop of light
more intimate, more bright
light is the splendor of the night
night as the backbone and foil for light
dark and shining: shining and dark
a night coat of gleaming sparks
that shine on us in the dark
light is flat without night
so come, sister not sinister night
give height in depth and glow
and a sisterly mystery to light

WATER

45

Biomes

marsh
garrigue
maquis
phrygana
pantano
tomillar
matorral
batha
chaparral
marais
فيضان
chamizal
Moor
fynbos
mallee
moss
طحلب
palude
maremma
مستنقع
swamp
سبخة
fen
pocosin
quag
salina
ملّاحة ـ
slough
wold

P.S. Historically most human settlements, and hence cultures, seem to have begun near swamps and rivers, to enjoy both fish and fowl. Transportation, and above all, water.

By Wave Express

> *As trees are by their bark embraced*
> *Love to my soul doth cling.*
> ~John Wilmot, 2nd Earl of Rochester

My river
doesn't want tears
—enough water, thank you
and no salt, please—
My river floats me
supports my dreams
and ferries new ones
by wave express
My river moves me gently
along the shores of life
that pass before my eyes

I shall remain tied to
my river by a trickle
This umbilical cord
doesn't want my tears

This is water
from a natural source
—Isn't all?
—Isn't love?

But I wonder where you go
pointing to the countries
in my chest
when you disappear
underground inside me

into the maps of faraway trees
the barks
the mangroves of desire
and where down there
we shall meet

Travel Brochure

*To the victims of the Costa Concordia
cruise accident on Jan 26, 2012*

Who will guarantee
that I find a sunset like that
gilding water flats on the beach
with yellow haloes all around
the waves?

And me riding on a tall camel?

And who will vouch that I shall face
weeping cherry blossoms
right there with me alone
with maybe just one
decorative Japanese woman
in a kimono
in the background?

Who promises me that a hale man
will put his arm around my shoulders
with plumeria blossoms and aromas
wafting all around?

A picture is worth a thousand words
a picture is worth a thousand lies
your promises made not to be fulfilled
your dreams are to be exploited only. And yet
as always when I travel
I will be in for a surprise or two:
Let them be pleasant

January/February 2012

NOTE: *This poem is not just about the uncertainty of travel. It speaks of the abyss between the claims of travel agencies and the often paltry realities of tourism, of which the Costa Concordia disaster is a glaring example. It excoriates the exploitation of eroticism in travel photos and the reduction of the "natives" to picturesque extras. It refers to the cherry blossoms in Japan, which, instead of promised solitary contemplation, have become mob events.*

Even in the Rain

Mouth he remembered: the quaint orifice
~ John Crowe Ransom

Your brown eyes shine
      in your beaming face
           ringed by drops of water

Even in the rain
      that delicious life of
           streets and windows sparkling

in an odd sideways light

Even in the rain
      steady holds your breath
           exhaling steamboat vapor

The magic of
      remembered dance motions
           carried on in a dream

So glad you're here
      you wear a shiny smile
           that lights up the street

and me and mine

As I Look Back

at the ME person
before I knew you, my love
I wonder if she
wasn't someone else

Someone marked by
lack and absence
by many Withouts
by barely rimmed Withins
by out-of-breath driven emotions
an abundance of frozen routines

Was she/I even whole?

Then you came
you came at me
you made me soar and swim
happy as fish in water
I like the way I am now

Thank you
for getting me wet

Aunt

In the garden
among the high grass
my aunt shimmers
as she walks

The sun has seized her
etching her against the sky
an aura surrounds her shadow

Her walk is in waves
her steps moist
on the damp earth

As if the air
had become water
fluid to the gaze

She is a walking
photograph, filtered
and unfixed

She is the dream
of herself I carry
with me to America

Unraveled — Sfilacciata

When I travel
it's just me I unravel
as if I were a sweater
that chose to be unmade
Naked even just surviving
half wanting to
half made to do it
Taking a deep breath
of the new and the other
losing myself in it
and finding just me

Me in the here and there
fresh among the unknown
new green just sprouted
me left alone and left over
breathing light and delight
[Maybe Penelope had
this secret of eternal life]

Sfilacciata

Quando viaggio
C'è solo me
sviaggiata sfilacciata
[come fossi un maglione
e avessi scelto di essere disfatto]
Nuda anche appena superstite
[metà volente metà costretta]
tirando un respiro profondo
dalle nuove cose e dalle altre
perdendomi in esse
e trovando solo a me

Solo io qua e là
fresca fra le cose
rimasta lasciata sola
respirando la leve luce
[Forse Penelope aveva
questo segreto della vita eterna]

Translated by Rita Stanzione

Travel Envy
or
My Wildest Dreams

In my dream you told me
you had been in Brazil
had gone to China
and seen the Fiji Islands
Samoa and Tahiti

You were in New Zealand
Venezuela and Colombia
and I only in Chile
You had been everywhere
in Africa and I hadn't
I felt intensely jealous

When I woke up
I realized I had traveled
to more places than you
Mexico Ecuador Scotland
Morocco Albania Portugal
Argentina Angkor Wat and and
not counting internet junkies

The times are a-changing
fifty years ago
"buried deep in Amazon"
meant the river
today it means the Internet

Like a Reed

Let every breeze
caress you in passing
let it sweep your skin
rake your bones
let every breeze
sweep right through you

Hold your body like a reed
slightly inclined
against the wind
aligned in a voyage
slightly voyant
and slightly blind
but forever floating
on the enveloping breeze

Writing on Water

Rêvant de cette société/ où tous auront loisir d'écrire.
Dreaming of a society/ where all would have the leisure to write.
~ *Guillevic*

After I beat the ink to pieces
on the tablet
I drop the bits like letters
on the watery sheet
one by one
I write myself on water
spread myself thin on the surface
see bleeding shadows descend
waving and wafting
deep into the water world

Becoming algae and fish
the creatures of water
released from my mind
set out on a new life
a watery freedom
a run of their own
mending the tear in the fabric
forming of my words
underwater gardens
tribute to becoming again
a part of nature

Music of Reflected Light

Tout s'en va, tout passe, l'eau coule, et le coeur oublie.
~ Gustave Flaubert

*I wander among
wandering sand dunes,
together we err
between land and sea*

If water is music, then earth is silence.

*Wasser weiß zu reden.
Water knows how to speak.
Ingeborg Bachmann*

**wavering mirror
water unites and we see
life and life of dreams**

ART

Transcript

Transplant

—— On an anonymous 14ᵗʰ century Italian painting

True art is to practice irreality.   ~Lovis Corinth

Cosmas and Damian,
the doctor saints
in red robes and tall hats
replaced the crippled man's
leg. He was white

They took a black man's leg
to underscore their skill: is it
one suffering, one flesh?

A prayer for the dead
is a prayer for the living?

The black man had been dead,
the white was alive
a skin-deep checkerboard
difference

> The question remains:
> Was there equality?
> Were there any
> living Blacks
> with grafted
> legs of
> white men
> to stand
> and to
> walk
> on
> their
> newly acquired
> white feet ??

NOTE: *The last stanza is supposed to represent a leg. Apollinaire revived such Calligrams popular in the Hellenistic and Baroque periods.*

Joaquín Sorolla

This painter knows water
Two men riding oxen through the waves
A little girl eagerly looking out to sea
A youth leading a horse through the surf
Muscular man breaking wet mussels off a rock
Little girl walking the surf's mirrored sheet
Two women guiding a boy across the sand
A wading boy floating a wooden sailboat
Two young ladies in white, the color of dunes
Two girls, one naked one dressed, lying in the wet
A mother holding up a towel to a dripping daughter
Girl leading her younger sister towards the sea
Man wrapping a wet woman in a huge sheet
to make love to her in an auspicious moment
Girl treading water with her younger brother

Bodies surrounded by air in a naked space
caught in the moment of their mortality

Titian—Titans at Work

The Dresden Venus and the friendship between Giorgione and Titian

His friend now dead
—Giorgione—
had painted the Venus
and now she lay
naked and dead
in his dark bottega

[An unfinished painting
that no one sees is a dead one]

So Titian the Titan
looked at her with open eyes
he took her out into the sun
and saw her for the first time
he devised a solution
and painted and painted

Nude woman is nature
no pretext needed
below he couched her body
in silk and satin
above he followed her contours
with a double landscape
first the dark hills
then a transparent distance
and above them alluring clouds

Harmonious whole
a tribute to friendship
an ode to nude beauty
a love shared by two men
See this woman fully human
desired as second nature

Giorgio Morandi

I stand in the museum
before some paintings
vases bottles carafes
and more
bottles carafes and vases

Nothing but
bottles vases and carafes
really

The art of silence
I imagine sitting quietly
in someone's living room
these objects present
against white walls
to feel the tranquility they exude
enjoy their art of silence

Human handiwork
reverting close to stone
to silent clay or stone
[Chardin comes to mind]

Morandi
a painter who paints
nothing but silence
the possible silence
the silence of my gaze
and yours
possible among us
and this is his gift:

Our lost silence
shaped in clay and
put on the shelf

Munch's New Snow

The street is a trough
lit by the carpeted snow
from below
and darkened by trees
clearly poplars and birches
botanically eloquently clear
[thank you Munch].
Their latent wintry hebetude
raring to go into spring.
Whenever!
Two people
muffled to the nines
walking out of the picture
in front.
It could be us
holding
gloved hands.

New Snow, painting by Edvard Munch

Munch's Winter

The time is winter,
a world that becomes
cracked, transparent,
brittle and cold.
Simpler also the outlines,
the colors muffled,
voluble grey-and-white masses,
above and before them
cross-hatched drawings
of twigs and branches,
as if by an austere artist
who sparingly renders
life in frozen black and white.
The painter understands winter,
scratched and voluminous
stands the stolid landscape,
waiting in a leaden patience,
waiting drop by drop
for spring.

Winter, painting by Edvard Munch

Klee's Moonlight

A luminous blue creamy and light
like looking into a blooming artichoke

Panels of soft light partitioned
like dreams that may come when we have not yet
shuffled off this mortal coil

But think of blue the soft sheen of silk
of stories in morning air of hope and promise

Spaces of light spaces of trees sun and the ambiguous
flat spaces that absorb it fighting blocks of dark

Slanted towards a hazy future
ours for the taking the wanting the hoping

Brancusi 'Sleeping Muse'

Lucid sleeper
resting upon herself
cushioned on air

Resplendent forehead
replenishing lips
luminous split

Like a peach
open to a wisp of thought
the smile of a dream

A fluid kiss of light
Eternity resting in
one glorious moment

'Muse endormie'

Dormeuse lucide
repliée en elle-même
couchée sur l'air

Front lumineux
lèvres abondantes
émaillées de joie

Comme une pêche
ouvertes au frisson d'une pensée
le sourire d'un rêve

Baiser fluide de lumière
une éternité reposant dans
un moment glorieux

Tanslated by Margaret Saine

Diebenkorn, Two Tomato Halves With a Knife On a Board

Two tomato halves
alone and separate
on the board
separated by a blade
surrounded by light and shadow
looking over the edges
of their wooden world
140

...نصفي ثمرة طماطم
...وحيدتان و منفصلتان بسكين
...محاطتان بالنور و الظل
...تنظران لحافة اللوحة
عالمهم الخشبي

Translated by Mohamed N. Elramady

PS: *Thank you so much for your translation, dear Mohamed, of course the Bing re-translation of your precious translation is a hopeless travesty, so I must take yours on faith [heart emoticon]. Mohamed N. Elramady is a poet who lives in Alexandria, Egypt.*

Constable Says

The world is wide

No two days are alike

I should paint my own places best

I run after pictures

I have done a good deal of skying

The sky is the chief organ of sentiment
in a painting

And never two leaves were alike
since the days of creation

Painting is but another word for feeling

*P.S. These are words from the journal of the great
British landscape painter, John Constable, 1776-1837.*

LAST SONGS

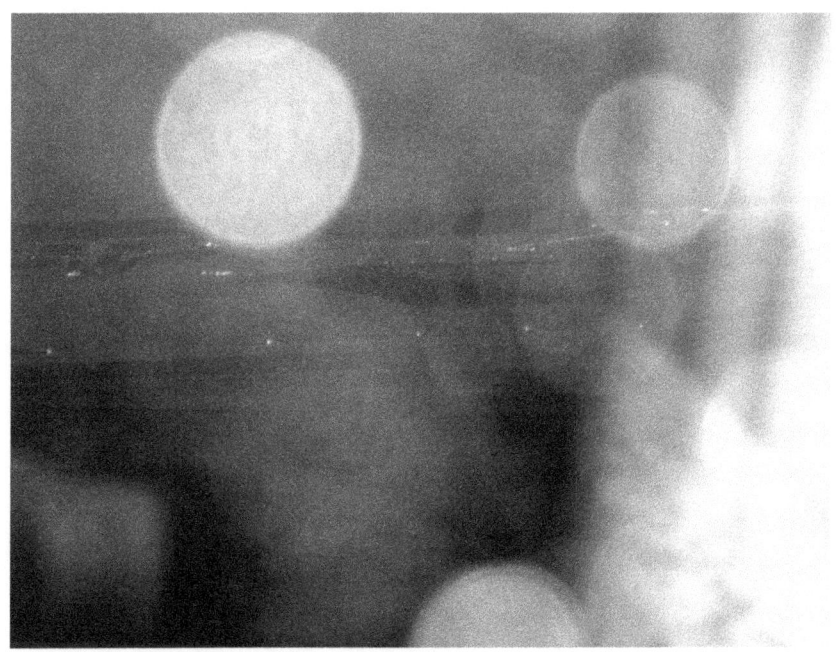

The Qasida of Creation

We hear the air sing
inside the flute
and under fingers that strum
the strings of the lute
the voices of our lives
rise and descend

A single flower grows
among roses and thorns
creating a wide garden
to please and welcome

A single drop of water
flows among others
to wash and ferry along
rivers watering the lands

The notes of a trill
rise and combine
a sweet music of the soul
to embrace and envelop

Three fish and
three breads multiply
in a banquet of love

Floating words
ferment and fuse bubbling sounds
from which a story is born
the voices of our lives
rise blend and descend

A wind that has spoken
is suddenly calm
and death falls silent
for a brief moment

Curtain Call

When the night
dropped her dark curtain
of eyelids between us
your velvet dreams
surged in my mind's eye

I am still with your old words
comforting as honey
words I cannot forget
that saved my life
when I found it
bleak and wanting

Now at daybreak
you and I are nothing
but two skins
warm as bread
touching so close
that your hands
wake my body and
mine caress yours

For Ulalume González de León

If trees could fly
—but they do—
they are islands
for birds
their leaves are flying birds
and their foliage
an immense humming
waving and weaving of wings
that take to the winds
carrying their lights
and shadows lightly
off into the skies to kiss
clouds with a meaning

P.S. *Ulalume González de León was a great Mexican poet born in Uruguay to her mother, Sara de Ibáñez, who was another great poet.*

Horizons

We are all
each other's species

Caught in a confused web
of fact and feeling

Lands thought safe and secure
have drifted and absconded

We are stories of sentiment
with occasional bits of truth

A sediment pierced by sunrays
over the morning horizon

In whose embrace we
arise from sleep

Groping vaguely forward
into a new day a second look

I want to be your deep down under
evening embrace

Your Calypso promise darling
on the daring side of love

We are all
each other's species

Breadcrumbs

I love breadcrumbs
and pick them
from wherever they land
tablecloths, sofas, my chest
you name it

I once read that
breadcrumbs are for the gods
If so how nice they have
good taste like me

If so on second thought
they might be angry
that I rob their crumbs

I sincerely hope
there is a goddess among them
who will smile at my folly
and placate the others
into forgiving me
for stealing their crumbs

Early Spring

> *the whole poem:*
> *a geometry of blood and phoneme*
> Corsino Fortes

Words deploy
like images in light
balloons of sighs to float
photograms of smiles

A give and a take
during the sunlit hours
a splash of words
seems natural as love

And sometimes time
remains suspended
between syllables

In a cloud of moments
a whirlpool of words
that doesn't want to pass

THE END

About the Author

Margaret Saine lives in Los Angeles. After a doctorate in French from Yale, she taught Spanish at universities in California and Arizona. She writes poetry, haiku, and short stories in five languages and also translates other poets. Her books are *Bodyscapes*, *Words of Art*, and five haiku chapbooks.

Poetry manuscripts ready for publication include *The Five Senses*, *Reading Your Lips*, *Words of Winter*, and *While Alive*, as well as *Paesaggi che respirano* [Breathing Landscapes], to be published in Italy. She has recently completed *As You Were Saying*, a dialogue with American poet William Carlos Williams.

www.ingramcontent.com/pod-product-compliance
Lightning Source LLC
Chambersburg PA
CBHW031205090426
42736CB00009B/786